The Durability of Cultural Influences: How American Foreign Policy Reinforced Historical Biases in El Salvador

A Monograph
by
Major Michael G Nelson
United States Air Force

School of Advanced Military Studies
United States Army Command and General Staff College
Fort Leavenworth, Kansas

AY 2008

SCHOOL OF ADVANCED MILITARY STUDIES

MONOGRAPH APPROVAL

Major Michael G Nelson

Title of Monograph: **The Durability of Cultural Influences: How American Foreign Policy Reinforced Historical Biases in El Salvador**

This monograph was defended by the degree candidate on 03 April 2008 and approved by the monograph director and reader named below.

Approved by:

_____   Monograph Director
Michael W. Mosser, Ph.D.

_____   Monograph Reader
Matthew T. Higginbotham, COL, QM

_____   Director,
Stefan J. Banach, COL, IN   School of Advanced
                                   Military Studies

_____   Director,
Robert F. Baumann, Ph.D.   Graduate Degree
                                   Programs

Abstract

THE DURABILITY OF CULTURAL INFLUENCES: HOW AMERICAN FOREIGN POLICY REINFORCED HISTORICAL BIASES IN EL SALVADOR by MAJOR Michael G Nelson, USAF, 53 pages.

A confluence of factors led to American engagement in one of Central America's most violent uprisings: the Salvadoran civil war. By the time of President Ronald Reagan's first term as president, the civil war had created social, political and economic fissures within the Salvadoran state; these fissures presented the United States the opportunity to promote its policy agenda with the Central American country. Reagan's administration, however, got off to a slow start; his first-term approaches to Salvadoran engagement yielded very little and may have actually exacerbated the negative influences affecting the state.

This monograph attempts to portray the American and El Salvadoran relationship during Reagan's first term as one defined by strategic interactions. These interactions occurred when American policy attempted to modify the Salvadoran system. Without delving into specific initiatives, the analysis will show how Reagan's administration was stimulated by distinct impulses, or influences, which not only encouraged engagement, but also molded policy. Among those influences, doctrinal precedents within the executive and the ideological leanings of President Reagan were the two areas that appeared to dominate Reagan's interaction with El Salvador. In order to succeed, theses influences would have to accommodate elements of Salvadoran history and culture, lest policy implementation fail.

Unfortunately neither of those influences encouraged the administration to obtain a full understanding of the situation prior to or during policy implementation. When American policy interacted with Central American history and culture, the resulting messages failed to resonate with the Salvadoran populace and efforts to change the system for the better fell flat. In the end, while the American administration interpreted its engagement as purely legitimate and rational, the Salvadoran body politic remained unconvinced the United States offered a better system of governance than the one at hand.

The American experience in El Salvador during Reagan's first term did create lessons learned that hold application beyond this specific case study. The administration's misapplication of ideological constructs and its inability to formulate a coherent strategy discouraged the introduction of any counterfactual information that might otherwise lead to a reframing of the perceived problem. That shortfall, combined with a cultural dissonance the United States could not overcome, conspired to eliminate chances for Salvadoran success during Reagan's first term.

TABLE OF CONTENTS

Introduction

In 1992, the Chapultepec Peace Accords officially ended one of the twentieth century's most violent civil wars. The extensiveness of the campaign, renowned for its violence, was magnified only by the diminutive size of the state in which it occurred. El Salvador had finally reached a point of relative peace.[1] Reaching that point required not only the efforts of its entire population, but also the involvement of the United States and other nations of the world. But the United States' intervention in El Salvador had not always resulted in measurable success, as demonstrated during the first term presidency of Ronald Reagan.

Historically, engagements between states have been plagued by the law of unintended consequences.[2] This inevitability is a product of human interaction and is particularly evident in dealings between states with long histories, as is the case between the United States of America and the countries of Central America. While the United States lacks a full measure of respectability within all of Central America, dealings with some states have proven to be particularly thorny in the recent past. Among these states is El Salvador, which makes this discussion all the more pertinent and relevant.

---

[1] The research for this monograph began with a soon-to-be-published article in *Military Review* entitled "Principles in Amnesty, Reconciliation and Reintegration: The Case for El Salvador." by Majors Michael Herrera and Michael Nelson.

[2] Note: Unintended consequences include those outcomes that either exceed the original intentions of, or fall outside the scope of expectations for, a particular government policy. Foreign policy practices may create unintended consequences in several ways. In the case of American engagement in El Salvador, the administration attempted to satisfy competing domestic agendas, invariably leading to a confusion of policy means with policy end states. Thomas Carothers refers to this as Reagan's "instrumentalization of prodemocracy policies," whereby American policymakers viewed establishment of democracy in El Salvador as both a means and an end state. See Thomas Carothers, "Promoting Democracy and Fighting Terror," *Foreign Affairs*, January/February 2003, http://www. foreignaffairs.org/20030101faessay10224-p20/thomas-carothers/promoting-democracy-and-fighting-terror html [accessed 15 February 2008].

1

This monograph will show how Reagan's first-term presidency saw its Salvadoran engagement plagued by what was recognized at the time as less-than-optimum outcomes – namely, the inability to defeat the communist insurgents and ensuring continued state control under a friendly regime.[3] Despite the best of intentions, Ronald Reagan's policies during the early 1980s were counterproductive to finding common ground with the Salvadorans in their fight against those communist insurgents.

As a counterbalance to the ideologically-founded insurgents, the Reagan administration used both doctrinal and ideological grounding to guide early Salvadoran policy initiatives. These factors, however necessary to instigate action on the part of the president, misguided administration initiatives to the extent that American foreign policy played into and reinforced preexisting cultural biases. Viewing Reagan policy positions from within the lens of Salvadoran culture helps explain how American foreign policy met with mixed success in El Salvador during the president's first administration.[4]

Bounding the discussion is a key component to proving this point. The most pertinent questions to answer include: What historical factors are relevant to understanding how US foreign policy and Salvadoran domestic policy interacted? What forces at play within the Reagan administration governed early implementation of its El Salvador policy? Did these forces oppose or reinforce historical biases within El Salvador? Although numerous other questions also exist, this monograph will focus only on the three mentioned above. These three were chosen because they lie at the base of any macro analysis of this issue; the answers to these questions will provide

---

[3] Laurence Whitehead. "Explaining Washington's Central American Policies," *Journal of Latin American Studies* 15, no. 2 (Nov. 1983): 329. Note: Hindsight has made the record less clear, with some administration supporters claiming that the Salvadoran policy 'failures' of the Reagan administration were a necessary part of the maturation of the peace process.

a basis for understanding the fundamental interaction between the United States and El Salvador and inevitably frame any future policy-specific discourse. Moreover, due to considerations of length, this monograph will only answer the three guiding questions to the extent those answers are germane to the thesis; in effect, completely answering the questions posed would require inordinate time and resources given the scope of this project.

Narrowing the monograph scope was challenging as well, if for no other reason than the sheer volume of information available. This monograph is not intended to be all-inclusive, but instead provide a focused example of how factors emerging from within the American system played a role in the eventual misdirection of Salvadoran policy. In other words, American domestic influences served as contributing factors to the continued destabilization of the Salvadoran state. Although a causal analysis is beyond the scope of this examination, a macro view of the American and Salvadoran context lends insight into the problem. In light of this consideration, this monograph provides a bridge between traditionally one-sided discussions, linking to some extent the policy cradle (influences) to the policy grave (resultant policy reverberations in El Salvador).

All of this relies on an accurate interpretation of the historical record. Interestingly, aside from the few exceptions noted below, surprisingly little counterfactual data exists for El Salvador during the civil war years. This fact speaks to one value of hindsight, as it has been applied since Reagan's first term over 25 years ago: though not always the case, the passing of time often allows for the reconciliation of cause and effect. Hindsight not only provides the breathing space needed to achieve a consolidated vision of past events, but at the same time the significance of

---

[4] William M. LeoGrande, "A Splendid Little War: Drawing the Line in El Salvador," *International Security* 6, no. 1 (Summer 1981): 46.

what happened often gives way to the greater question of why it happened. This monograph attempts to answer at least part of that question.

In all, an enormous amount of research has been conducted over the last 25 years on the subject of American engagement with El Salvador in the early 1980s. Despite the wealth of information on the issue, some counterfactual commentary continues to this day. Responsibility for many acts of violence, especially those that seized public attention, is still unclear. Suspicions have given way to unproven, but presumptive accusations of guilt; history (and the amnesty associated with the Peace Accords), however, has made that discussion largely irrelevant. The greatest issue still under contention appears to be the guerrillas desired end state. The underlying intentions of the guerrillas are often still clouded by rhetoric. During the time frame relevant for this discussion (roughly late1979 to early 1985), many of the guerillas' individual views contradicted commentary from official entities operating under the broad umbrella guerrilla group known as the Farabundo Martí National Liberation Front (FMLN). The clearest reason for this dissension may be organizational in nature: For some time after the five major groups merged in 1980, leaders continued to advertise their own group-specific ideologies and biases rather than sticking to a program of approved FMLN talking points. Examples of this dissension can be found in writings and commentary of the guerilla leaders; the FMLN web page, which continues to thrive today; and in a host of other sources too numerous to mention. In any event, this monograph obviates the need to resolve this issue by focusing instead on the impact American policy had on the recognized Salvadoran government.

As far as the literary record is concerned, the history complied by Max G. Manwaring and Court Prisk provided the most comprehensive list of primary sources available, all of whom had direct knowledge of or experience with the subject matter. Comprehensive raw commentary from many of those same sources is limited elsewhere, leaving little discretion but to use what is readily available. Although clearly a single source – and an edited one at that –Manwaring's book still provides a wealth of data from a variety of reputable people.

In addition to primary sources, there exists an overwhelming amount of secondary and editorial writings. This monograph uses selected peer-reviewed journals and books written during the civil war to emphasize the notions of the time while at the same time avoiding excessive commentary obtained through hindsight. While the use of contemporary sources was not completely restricted, their use was limited to specific instances where the value of hindsight was deemed to outweigh any bias they may have contributed.

Beyond the oral history noted above, material on this subject generally falls into one of two categories, with either an American-centric or Salvadoran-centric read on events. While both approaches contribute to the discourse admirably, they fail to bridge the gap so to speak. They all relate events as they happened, and yet the reasons why the war in El Salvador seemed to stagnate during Reagan's first term remain unclear. American-centric literature reports on the process of policymaking within the American administration, focusing on the frictions and alliances necessary to see policy come to fruition, but fails to follow through on evaluating the effectiveness of that policy. Salvadoran-centric literature highlights the reverberations of policy actions within the Salvadoran state, but fails to trace back the influences that generated such policy in the first place. The centric approach not only fails to tell the whole story, but oftentimes draws conclusions that are misleading. Observing the interaction between America and El Salvador in the early 1980s using a centric model provides, in effect, only one side of the story.

American-centric approaches are aptly represented by William LeoGrande's book, *Our Own Backyard*. While cited infrequently, the book provided a wealth of contextual information and situational understanding. LeoGrande's book offers a comprehensive look at domestic policy approaches during the Reagan administration – one far superior to what this monograph could offer – but it focuses more on frictions within the Reagan team during policy development and employment rather than on how its policy themes rippled into and affected the Salvadoran context.

An example of the Salvadoran-centric approach is provided by Clifford Krauss in his book *Inside Central America*. Krauss takes a markedly more regional approach, succinctly reporting what took place during the years in question, but his book provides little linkage back to policy motivations from the American standpoint. His book, though valuable, reads more like a Central Intelligence Factbook by rendering the briefest of looks into complex situations. This monograph takes the opposite approach and tries to keenly focus on very specific subject matter: the overt influences that helped shape American policy initiatives during Reagan's first term and how those themes resonated in the Salvadoran context.

Walter LaFeber's book, *Inevitable Revolutions: the United States in Central America,* is another example of a regional analysis, but his writing more closely resembles a more balanced look at both sides of the equation (hereafter the 'bridge' or 'bridging' approach). A book of comprehensive history, LaFeber's book delves into the discordant beliefs and rationales found within various American administrations throughout years of Central American engagement. His book highlights both the inadequacies of policy as well as the inhospitable environments into which they were injected, thereby qualifying as a bridging vehicle.

This monograph deviates from LaFeber's work in two critical aspects. First, LaFeber's research serves only historical needs: he draws very few, if any, general principles from American engagement in Central America. Instead, LaFeber leaves the reader to drawn their own parallels to current and future policy actions, leaving open the possibility of contradictory interpretations. Furthermore, his approach argues the United States consciously sought to keep Central American nations under the umbrella of economic dependency and exercised control to that end from afar.[5] This monograph shows that engagement in Central America may not have been as voluntary as he claims; it was a natural, rational outgrowth of influences within American political precedent and the president himself. Indeed, rather than viewing the engagement as a function of economic dependency, a more pertinent discussion might entail which was less voluntary, the engagement itself or the policy form it took.

Other bridge commentary also exists. Enrique Baloyra, in particular, has written a large quantity of articles central to this theme. His closest parallel to this paper, *Central America on the Reagan Watch: Rhetoric and Reality* (Journal of Interamerican Studies and World Affairs, Feb, 1985) focuses more on the juxtaposition of American goals and methods in Central America and not on the particulars of how engagement as a whole reinforced preexisting cultural biases. His research further reduces its scope to focus on policy-specific approaches, whereas due to its nature, this monograph tries to emphasize more strategic concepts.

In keeping with this strategic approach, the ensuing discussion will focus on relevant areas of American and Salvadoran history. Despite the fact both countries have been intimately involved with one another for some time, they do not share a broad common history; indeed, had the two countries been party to similar shared experiences, the chances for misunderstanding and misapplication of intent during Reagan's first administration would greatly diminish. In some fashion, the lack of qualitative interaction in the past set the stage for fundamental miscalculations in foreign policy during the early 1980s. Comparisons and contrasts do exist, but for the most part these histories will be reviewed as discrete elements.

---

[5] Robert A. Pastor, "Explaining U.S. Policy Toward The Caribbean Basin: Fixed and Emerging Images," *World Politics* 38, no. 3 (April 1986): 490-491.

Roots of the Conflict

Modern Salvadoran history can be traced back until approximately 1850. At the time, the government was concerned about the country's reliance upon a single crop, indigo. The intensive effort to diversify agricultural products swung the economic pendulum so dramatically toward the new crop, coffee, that it replaced indigo as the primary cash crop for the country. Since this new product was a land-intensive venture, nearly all arable land fell under the specter of coffee, creating enormous wealth for those who could exploit its potential. As a secondary outflow, the resultant rich-poor gap also transcended the economic realm into the political one, leading to a perceived sense of entitlement and elitism. The groups fortunate enough to prosper from coffee, known as the fourteen families, used their influence and wealth to modernize the state and unite the government of El Salvador.

The Salvadoran government became one of Latin America's first to rise without the assistance of a single dictator; instead, its strength lay in the support of the newly established oligarchy.[6] Although the national government existed more to facilitate the wishes of the oligarchy, it remained effectively unchallenged for nearly 100 years, due in great part to the skyrocketing value and demand for coffee on the world stage. It seems what was good for the oligarchy – increased revenue – was also good for those working the land (the campesinos), despite the fact they benefitted indirectly at best.

Unfortunately, the economic ascendency of the oligarchy brought with it societal fractures that would eventually wreak havoc on El Salvador. Land was increasingly horded by the fourteen families, which continued to create one of the most significant rich/poor gaps in all of Latin America. Even as late as 1974, the top one percent of families made more than the poorest fifty percent combined.[7] Steep economic divisions also prevented the creation of a viable middle class. In fact, during the period of 1910-1914, coffee exports represented almost 87 percent of the average value of all Salvadoran exports.[8] For nearly 150 years, the coffee plantation remained synonymous with wealth and power in El Salvador.

During this same period, the United States faced few of the same challenges. Neither geography nor government limited the potential for economic advancement. Relative to that of El Salvador, the geography of the United States offered its people an almost unbounded agricultural potential. Even as a newly-recognized country, the United States' land mass overshadowed that of El Salvador; by the beginning of El Salvador's modern era (1850), the size of the United States had further increased to include states as far south as Texas and as far west as California. Furthermore, federalism and the emphasis on individual freedoms allowed nearly all citizens to exploit the advantages of unrestricted commerce. Though slavery, the lack of universal suffrage and other ailments continued to vex American society, even those structural impediments to upward mobility paled in comparison to the ones that bound Salvadoran society.

The economic ailment particular to the Salvadoran society originated with the non-uniform distribution of wealth, combining a finite number of rich people with a general populace of few means. While this extreme economic exclusion would have a lesser impact in a country full of resources and/or opportunities for advancement, El Salvador hardly ever fit this mold. By the 1930s, only 10% of the population of El Salvador owned all of the land. This drastic

---

[6] Enrique A. Baloyra, *El Salvador in Transition.* (Chapel Hill, N.C.: University of North Carolina Press, 1983); 5.

[7] Walter LaFeber, *Inevitable Revolutions: The United States in Central America.* exp. ed. (New York: W.W. Norton, 1984), 243.

[8] Enrique A. Baloyra, *El Salvador in Transition.* (Chapel Hill, N.C.: University of North Carolina Press, 1983); 6.

distribution of resources burdened disenfranchised Central Americans to the extent that it acted to prevent a groundswell of opposition to the oligarchy. Peter Singelmann claims that "…scarcity and dependence in the rural community gave rise to conflict and competition among the campesinos while at the same time encouraging the establishment of particularistic loyalties between individual campesinos and their patron, at the expense of class solidarity."[9]

Though Singelmann continues to detail how this affliction cast a shadow over the entire region and not just the Salvadoran state, El Salvador may have suffered most: by the mid-eighties it had become known as the poorest country in Central America. El Salvador's Gross Domestic Product (GDP) from 1950 was equal to its real per capita GDP in 1982.[10] Even as of 2002, 48% of the populace lived in poverty[11], demonstrating that economic progress is slow in coming. The fact that El Salvador maintains the second-highest GDP in Central America is not as much a testament to the success of their economic policies, as it is an indictment of other regional countries' economic patterns.[12]

The economic success – and in many ways the societal fabric – of El Salvador relied upon the stability of the coffee market. Falling worldwide demand for coffee as well as competition from other producers precipitated the downfall of the Salvadoran economy. This created friction among the poor and their patrons, leading to the organization of some grass roots groups bent on the redress of grievances. Nonetheless, the oligarchy, by this time using the

---

[9] Peter Singelmann, "Campesino Movements and Class Conflict in Latin America: The Functions of Exchange and Power," *Journal of Interamerican Studies and World Affairs* 16, no. 1 (Feb. 1974): 43.

[10] Bulmer-Thomas, Victor. "Economic Development Over the Long Run – Central America Since 1920," *Journal of Latin American Studies*, 1983: 276.

[11] Kevin Sullivan, "El Salvador: On Unfinished Road to Reform; Despite Being Hailed by US as a Success Story, Economic Problems Persist," *Washington Post*, March 24, 2002.

[12] Economist Intelligence Unit ViewsWire. *El Salvador: Ten-year growth outlook*. New York, July 13, 2007.

military to ensure its continued control of the state,[13] struggled to retain power over an increasingly uncompetitive country with progressively fewer chances to recover from economic ruin. Methods utilized by the oligarchy to ensure continued compliance of the population included open oppression of minorities and even overt corruption.[14].

Diminishing prosperity and a booming population in the latter half of the nineteenth century further contributed to a breakdown in political consensus.[15] By the 1960s, what Walter LaFeber described as one of Central America's "inevitable revolutions" began.[16] The 1970s saw disparate communist forces well-entrenched in the rural areas of El Salvador attempting to dislodge a government that owed allegiance to alternatively, the oligarchy, then the army. By the time violence stopped in the early 1990s, the war between the El Salvador Armed Forces and the groups that eventually coalesced into the FMLN killed 75,000 civilians and left 8,000 missing.[17] In the years leading up to the peace accords in 1992, the conflict bogged down, with Nicaragua and Cuba supporting the rebels and the United States on the side of the Salvadoran government. Neither the FMLN nor the government forces could muster enough offensive strength to win decisively so increasingly battles were fought using irregular forces who demonstrated little compunction for the rights of civilians.

---

[13] Max G. Manwaring and Court Prisk, *El Salvador at War: An Oral History of Conflict from the 1979 Insurrection to the Present* (Washington, D.C.: National Defense University Press, 1988), 14.

[14] Tommie Sue Montgomery, *Revolution in El Salvador: From Civil Strife to Civil Peace.* 2nd ed. (Boulder: Westview Press, 1995), 65.

[15] Max G. Manwaring and Court Prisk, *El Salvador at War: An Oral History of Conflict from the 1979 Insurrection to the Present* (Washington, D.C.: National Defense University Press, 1988), 16-17.

[16] Walter LaFeber, *Inevitable Revolutions: The United States in Central America.* exp. ed. (New York: W.W. Norton, 1984), 16.

[17] Clifford Krauss, "The Salvadoran Quagmire," *Inside Central America* (New York: Touchstone 1999), 55.

The United States suffered from its own civil war nearly 150 years before the outbreak of the Salvadoran conflict, but that simple parallel does not justify any analogy between the two. Differences between the conflicts significantly outweigh any similarities, making the two events contextually dissimilar. For example, conventional wisdom cites the proximate cause of the American Civil War as the battle over states' rights. While the Salvadoran rebels' agenda demanded a radical shift in the political formula for government, neither side in the American Civil War sought a departure from their chosen political model. Instead, the dispute between the American states was based on divergent interpretations of the federalist model of government and not on its utility.[18] Rather than serving as a referendum on political ideology, the conflict actually helped clarify and strengthen the resident form of American government by defining the boundaries for national, state and individual rights. And although the uneven peace that followed the Civil War disrupted societal norms, American society could still cling to some stabilizing forces: the political model of government was unchanged and economic opportunity persisted. At no time before, during or after its conflict did El Salvador enjoy similar stabilizing forces.[19] In particular, the early 1980s proved to be some of the most trying of times, as the country and its people were forced to endure upheavals in the political, economic and social realms.

Even a cursory overview of political, economic and social influences shows how they were finely interwoven into Salvadoran history. Not only does its history speak to the expectation of a strong central government, but perhaps more importantly, to the need to exercise strength in order to govern. So much of the cultural identity of El Salvador is defined by a deep-

_____

[18]Marshall L. DeRosa, *The Confederate Constitution of 1861: An Inquiry into American Constitutionalism*, (Columbia, Missouri: University of Missouri Press, 1991), 7.

[19] Note: For an expanded discussion on the manifestation of this characteristic in El Salvador and other countries, see the series beginning with Dr. Michael W. Mosser's "The Armed Reconciler: The

rooted class division between the economic and politically elite and the impoverished working

class that upward social mobility – especially in the early 1980s – was nearly nonexistent.[20]

Class distinction and the resultant oppression created the near-equivalent of a caste system: "El

Salvador is today [1985] what it always has been: a nation of betrayal and terror, where military

strongmen, wealthy oligarchs, and village thugs seek final solutions of one political extreme or

another"[21]. This perception was generally sanctioned and accepted as fact by all levels of

Salvadoran society in the late 1970s, providing the context into which Ronald Reagan would

attempt to introduce his new policies.

Reagan Administration Foreign Policy Influences

The American presidential elections of 1980 swept President Reagan into office with a

clear mandate for change. Determined to complete a broad shift in Central American policy,

President Reagan chose to mold his policy from motivations distinctly different than those of

President Carter. In fact, a substantial part of his party plank cited key differences between his

and the ex-president's Central America posture. In particular, Reagan disagreed with returning

the Panama Canal to local control, claimed there was no need to apologize for past (mis)deeds in

Central America, and professed a desire to focus on "…reasserting glory of the country [US]"

through decisive policy in the Western Hemisphere and around the world.[22]

Military Role in the Amnesty, Reconciliation and Reintegration Process," *Military Review* (November-December 2007), 13-19.

[20]Elisabeth Jean Wood, *Forging Democracy from Below.* (Cambridge: Cambridge University Press, 2000), 6-7.

[21] Clifford Krauss, "The Salvadoran Quagmire," *Inside Central America* (New York: Touchstone 1999), 57.

[22] Laurence Whitehead, "Explaining Washington's Central American Policies," *Journal of Latin American Studies* 15, no. 2 (Nov. 1983): 327.

Chief among his attempts to distance himself from Carter was Reagan's engagement strategy for El Salvador. While the United States would continue to actively insert itself into domestic Salvadoran politics as it did under Carter, its dealings would be modified to reflect the motivations of the president and his close advisors. As such, it is instructive to first try and frame these motivations in order to understand how his chosen methods of engagement may or may not have achieved his visualization of success in the Salvadoran state.

For the sake of clarity, Reagan's foreign policy rationale will be categorized under two capstone concepts: doctrinal and ideological impulses. While some of the driving forces behind his Salvadoran policy surely fall outside these bounds, they are largely irrelevant to this discussion, as this monograph does not try to assign any one force as a causal variable to the outcomes found within the Salvadoran state. On the other hand, both doctrinal and ideological impulses did help define, shape and alter Reagan's approach to resolving the Salvadoran crisis.

Key to understanding the manner in which doctrinal and ideological concepts played into molding Reagan policy is to first understand how they related to each other. As will be seen, doctrinal precedents have served to reinforce the role of the United States as an arbiter, fair or otherwise, in the Western Hemisphere. Doctrinal precedent – the Monroe Doctrine and the Roosevelt Corollary are particularly relevant here –acted to imbue all United States presidents (not just Reagan) with the sense that the United States' role was that of a hemispheric policeman: crises demanded resolution, and resolution could only come with engagement from the US.

Meanwhile, Reagan administration ideologies also encouraged Salvadoran engagement. Due to their nature, however, these ideological impulses did not instill a need to intervene as did doctrinal impulses; more to the point, they conveyed the tone of the engagement rather than encouraging engagement itself. Since ideological grounds often convey a sense of certainty without offering a manner by which they can be disproven, target groups of ideologically-grounded policy may interpret it as paternalistic in nature. Even Richard Allen, the president's National Security Advisor, was quoted as saying "What we need is another Teddy Roosevelt,"[23] as if the Central Americans were wholly unable to deal with their situations without American intervention. This quote also implies a lack of historical knowledge of Central America by one of the president's chief advisors, since "revolutions have served the functions of elections in the United States" in that they transfer power and bring about change.[24] Whereas doctrinal precedents provided the 'we need to act' rationale for El Salvador engagement, the Reagan administration's ideological grounding conveyed the 'we know how to help' rationale of that engagement.

These symbiotic influences create a policy environment that is at the same time necessary and dangerous. It is necessary since any prospective engagement requires both a solution to a problem ('we know how to help') as well as the political will to institute the directed course of action ('we need to act'). Simultaneously, this environment may encourage an unintended effect: with an ideologically-based solution so readily in hand and a tendency to act, the resulting policy may preclude any perceived need to redefine or frame the problem on an ongoing basis. Part of that reframing requires questioning the validity of all aspects of the situation, to include individual or collective biases. In short, the danger inherent in ideologically-based policy is it may engender the proverbial solution in search of a problem. This became a key obstacle to American policy success in El Salvador.

---

[23] Walter LaFeber, *Inevitable Revolutions: The United States in Central America.* exp. ed. (New York: W.W. Norton, 1984), 274.

[24] Ibid., 15.

From a historical standpoint, the ideologically-based approach might be least likely to succeed in the long run, given the spotty record the United States has in the Central American region. Not only has the United States been accused of a heavy-handed approach in the region – Pfaff called it the "U.S. national predilection for carrying a big stick in Central America"[25] – but the relations themselves have been cyclical in nature.[26] This inevitably leads to the less-than-charitable though rational conclusion in Latin America that the United States involves itself in the region insofar as its own self interest is at stake. Despite the risks inherent with an ideological policy foundation, this standard served as one of the fundamental backbones to Reagan-era policy – perhaps even more so than traditional doctrinal influences.

Doctrinal Precedent

Doctrinal impulses in play included an evolving view of conventional, established policy as well as near-term positions taken up as recently as the Carter administration. The conventional doctrine process, set into motion by the Monroe Doctrine, experienced a maturation ending with Reagan. In combination with regional treaties noted below, these policies led the Reagan administration to be proactive in its dealings with El Salvador. During the presidential transition of 1980-1981, this tendency was only reinforced by the pre-existing US-Salvadoran conduits established by the Carter administration, which was also subject to the same doctrinal influences.

First and foremost of the formal policies, the Monroe Doctrine of 1823 staked out the Western Hemisphere as the United States' area of influence. The Doctrine was initially focused on old European powers (specifically France, Spain and to a smaller extent Russia), but had since

---

[25] William Pfaff, "U.S. Makes Mistakes when Ideology Prevails," *The Ottawa Citizen,* December 28, 1989.

[26] Gordon Connell-Smith, "Latin America in the Foreign Relations of the United States." *Journal of Latin American Studies* 8, no. 1 (May 1976): 138.

been interpreted as applicable to any nation or power not native to the Northern, Central or Southern America.[27] While communicating the idea that American national security was implicitly interlinked with the stability of its southern neighbors, the Monroe Doctrine did not provide a clear path for American involvement in those cases where instability did not arise from European interference. Instead, Monroe reiterated "…the true policy of the United States [is] to leave the parties [countries of the Western hemisphere] to themselves, in the hope that other powers will pursue the same course…."[28] In and of itself, the Monroe Doctrine provided one justification for American engagement into El Salvador insofar as the instability could be linked to a threat of US national security. The Roosevelt Corollary to Monroe's Doctrine, however, significantly eased the burden of proof for future administrations.

Theodore Roosevelt's Corollary to the Monroe Doctrine advanced the notion that it was America's "sole duty to protect life and property in the Western Hemisphere."[29] While the initial intent of the statement sought to protect the bankrupt Dominican Republic from European creditors, it has since been interpreted to expand the role of America as a hemispheric policeman. American presidents have also used it to justify unilateral interventions into select countries within Central and South America. While the Monroe Doctrine drew the line against European interference, the Roosevelt Corollary can be interpreted as having obligated the United States to act in the case of hemispheric instability irrespective of where that line fell. In a practical sense,

---

[27] United States Department of State's Bureau of International Information Programs, "Monroe Doctrine (1823)," United States Department of State International Information Programs, http://usinfo. state.gov/usa/infousa/facts/democrac/50.htm; [accessed November 16, 2007].

[28] Ibid..

[29] Jack Godwin, *The Arrow and the Olive Branch* (Westport, CT: Praeger Publishers). http://psi.praeger.com/doc.aspx?newindex=1&q=Monroe+Doctrine&c=&imageField.x=9&imageField.y=6 &d=/books/dps/2000accd/2000accd-p2000accd9970136001.xml&i=7.[accessed November 16, 2007].

the Roosevelt Corollary dismissed the need to establish European interference as a prerequisite for American involvement in the affairs of another state in the western hemisphere.

Post-World War II activities completed this maturation of American policy. The Rio Treaty of 1947 created a post-war collective security establishment specific to the Americas. Not only was this Treaty timely for several newly-independent nations of Central and South America, but it also obligated parties to provide "reciprocal assistance" in the case of insurgencies that threatened the peace – an oblique reference to address the fear generated by the upswing in communist insurgencies[30], a parallel recognized by the revolutionaries in El Salvador decades later.[31] Almost forty years later, President Reagan took this concept to its furthest interpretation: though not specific to the western hemisphere, the United States insisted it would actively oppose communist-supported insurgencies that threatened the status quo as well as offer "American moral and material support for insurgent movements attempting to oust Soviet-backed regimes...,"[32], a far cry from the initial intent of James Monroe back in 1823. (Under Reagan, material support would slant toward military support, but that discussion is beyond the scope of this paper.) From their relatively innocuous beginnings, doctrinal precedents up to and including the Reagan presidency moved American foreign policy vis-à-vis hemispheric intervention from a 'should' policy (Monroe Doctrine) to a 'could' policy (Roosevelt Corollary) to a 'would' policy (Reagan Doctrine).[33] This evolution was quite possibly unconscious and reflected an American

---

[29] C. G. Fenwick, "Procedure Under the Rio Treaty of Reciprocal Assistance." *The American Journal of International Law* 63, no. 4 (Oct. 1969): 769.

[31] Max G. Manwaring and Court Prisk, *El Salvador at War: An Oral History of Conflict from the 1979 Insurrection to the Present* (Washington, D.C.: National Defense University Press, 1988), 107.

[32]Ted Galen Carpenter, "U.S. Aid to Anti-Communist Rebels: The "Reagan Doctrine" and its Pitfalls," The Cato Institute, http://www.cato.org/pubs/pas/pa074es html. [accessed 21 November 2007].

[33] This progression of foreign policy thought was not linear, but rather a developing appreciation for what Americans expected – and would accept – from their government. Indeed, Roosevelt's actions in

philosophy that had lain latent until it could be fully expressed through the imposition of national means. Nonetheless, these collective doctrines defined the foreign policy environment within which Reagan's American policy in El Salvador would succeed or fail.

The last of these impulses for American policy in El Salvador emerged from precedent established under the Carter presidency. On the whole, policymakers believed continuity between the Carter and Reagan administrations was beneficial;[34] much like Reagan attempted in his later administration, the US under Carter had used a carrot-and-stick approach to enable the establishment of a Salvadoran centrist government. The establishment of a centrist government in El Salvador was key to the definition of success within both White Houses. Since both White Houses sought to establish a moderate Salvadoran government, one could say Reagan simply amplified Carter administration policies.[35] That conclusion, however, would ignore a significant difference in their respective underlying end states: President Carter's true policy cornerstone involved the resolution of human rights abuses,[36] while Reagan's policy dealt with winning what he saw as one battle in the greater East-West conflict between democracy and communism. For Reagan, however, so long as they did not inhibit his ability to engage in Salvadoran affairs, human rights took a distant back seat to ideological concerns until at least midway through his

---

South and Central America (as well as Wilson's before him) alone might indicate that his Corollary had pushed American policy to the 'would' stage, but Roosevelt's policy focused narrowly on those unstable countries that could not pay their foreign debt. I argue that this Corollary was forced upon him; otherwise the European powers had a clear path to interference in the Americas justified by the need to enforce debt payments owed to Continental powers. In contrast, Reagan took to his Doctrine willingly. His Doctrine also assumed a blatantly offensive position far greater than those feelings enumerated by Roosevelt.

[34] Max G. Manwaring and Court Prisk, *El Salvador at War: An Oral History of Conflict from the 1979 Insurrection to the Present* (Washington, D.C.: National Defense University Press, 1988), 98.

[35] Robert Pastor, "Continuity and Change in U.S. Foreign Policy: CARTER AND REAGAN ON EL SALVADOR." *Journal of Policy Analysis & Management* 3, no. 2 (Winter 1984): 181-182.

[36] "El Salvador Civil War," Global Security, http://www.globalsecurity.org/military/world/war/elsalvador2.htm [accessed November 21, 2007].

second administration.[37] The most glaring public admission of this position came in 1981, when Reagan abruptly dismissed Robert White, a critic of military-sponsored human rights abuses in El Salvador, from his post as Ambassador.[38]

Ideological Precedent

Within the Reagan administration, ideological grounding perhaps played the most fundamental role in policy formulation. Indeed, many of his policies, including but not restricted to the Reagan Doctrine, sprung forth from an unabashed certainty in his political ideals.[39] A strident anti-communist, Reagan's election was seen as a validation of core conservative values. From a narrow view, anti-communist rhetoric served to justify Reagan's view of Central America as a regional pawn. A wealth of data existed implicating rebels in El Salvador to similar factions in Nicaragua, Honduras and Costa Rica.[40] These links were continually used to validate the perceptions of the Reagan White House that the Salvadoran war was a small battle in the Great Game between the US and the Soviet Union.

In hindsight, several events substantiate these claims, though Reagan policy positions often communicated a level of concern somewhat divergent from the ground truth.[41] When ideological positions led him to believe in less-than-factual assertions, Reagan demonstrated how

---

[37] Tamar Jacoby, "The Reagan Turnaround on Human Rights," *Foreign Affairs*, http://www foreignaffairs.org/19860601faessay7802/tamar-jacoby/the-reagan-turnaround-on-human-rights html [accessed November 21, 2007].

[38] Margaret O'Brien Steinfels, "Death and Lies in El Salvador: The Ambassador's Tale," Creighton University, http://www.creighton.edu/CollaborativeMinistry/RbtWhite html [accessed December 20, 2007].

[39] Jerome Slater, "Dominos in Central America: Will they Fall? Does it Matter?" *International Security* 12, no. 2 (Autumn 1987): 106.

[40] Max G. Manwaring and Court Prisk, *El Salvador at War: An Oral History of Conflict from the 1979 Insurrection to the Present* (Washington, D.C.: National Defense University Press, 1988), 108.

his situational understanding could be stymied by preconceived notions. For example, his claim that regional communist actors played a key role in supporting the FMLN is only partially true: Castro himself was influential with FMLN leadership; in fact, the FMLN formed at his urging.[42] The full extent to which Castro, the Soviets or even the Nicaraguan Sandinistas actively supported the revolution in El Salvador, however, remains unclear to this day. In the end, although enough evidence exists to support Reagan's portrayal of El Salvador as a target of a worldwide communist conspiracy, considerable evidence also exists that indicates his first administration misinterpreted the situation in El Salvador out of loyalty to Reagan's unflinching anti-communist position[43].

Reagan's inner circle used a variety of pseudo-independent commissions and reports to bolster its claims that the Salvadoran problem was simply a small part of the communist plan for global conquest. Among the most public, the Kissinger Commission and the White Paper on El Salvador met with only mixed results. The White Paper, ostensibly 'proof' of Soviet regional influence (by, with and through the Nicaraguans and Cubans) was widely regarded as a lacking credibility.[44] Though the Kissinger Commission did not have to deal with questions of credibility, critiques of the commission's findings found it to be suspect for partisan reasons.[45]

---

[41] Walter LaFeber, *Inevitable Revolutions: The United States in Central America.* exp. ed. (New York: W.W. Norton, 1984), 276.

[42] Max G. Manwaring and Court Prisk, *El Salvador at War: An Oral History of Conflict from the 1979 Insurrection to the Present* (Washington, D.C.: National Defense University Press, 1988), 119.

[43] William M. LeoGrande, *Our Own Backyard : The United States in Central America, 1977-1992.* (Chapel Hill, NC: University of North Carolina Press, 1998). 214.

[44] Tommie Sue Montgomery, *Revolution in El Salvador: From Civil Strife to Civil Peace.* 2nd ed. (Boulder: Westview Press, 1995), 150. Note: For a more personal account, see Phillip Agee and Warner Poelchau, *White Paper Whitewash : Interviews with Philip Agee on the CIA and El Salvador.* (New York: Deep Cover Books, 1981).

[45] Jerome Slater, "Dominos in Central America: Will they Fall? Does it Matter?" *International Security* 12, no. 2 (Autumn 1987): 108.

Hindsight suggests that the administration used both of these sources to try and sway a dubious audience (Congress and the American people) to the president's position rather than as pillars of unbiased knowledge used to define original policy.[46]

Ultimately, judging the degree to which Reagan's ideological leanings coincided with the "ground truth" in El Salvador is irrelevant, though the above has demonstrated those leanings played a critical role in his policy formation. Similarly, arguing that ideological influences alone could not have spurred American involvement in Central America also misses the mark.[47] Instead, importance lies in the notion that ideological foundations for policy, in and of themselves, wed policymakers to positions such that they were loath to reconsider the facts, even if warranted by the situation.[48] The subtlety of this occurrence made it all the more dangerous: while willing to doubt information that challenges a declared position, Reagan himself was unlikely to reexamine his own biases as a source of flawed policy rationale.[49] Unfortunately for the case of El Salvador, this disinclination to consider all facets of overall engagement led the administration to support a policy that actually magnified cultural influences in a manner that contributed to the instability of the state.

The impact of both the doctrinal and ideological influences is evident. The Reagan team combined historical precedent with presidential guidance to develop Salvadoran policy. His

---

[46] Ibid., 110.

[47] Laurence Whitehead. "Explaining Washington's Central American Policies," *Journal of Latin American Studies* 15, no. 2 (Nov. 1983): 323.

[48] Ibid., 352.

[49] Shannon Lindsey Blanton suggests that Reagan's unwillingness to consider "discordant information" decreased over time. As the amount of evidence build up that placed his policies in doubt, she suggests, he became more and more open to the possibility that his Salvadoran policy was wrong. In her view, this transition took place late in his first administration (no earlier than 1984) and resulted from the cumulative effects of discordant information. See Shannon Lindsey Blanton, "Images in Conflict: The Case of Ronald Reagan and El Salvador." *International Studies Quarterly* 40, no. 1 (Mar. 1996): 38-39.

administration also established sound goals to measure success. Policy success, however, ultimately relied upon American logic that had yet to withstand the scrutiny of a foreign environment experiencing un-American conditions. In short, Reagan's first administration spun his Salvadoran policy around American-centric rationale; their approach and understanding to the Salvadoran problem did not prepare them for what was to come.

Salvadoran Engagement: Obstacles to Success

> "...*each time the United States has attempted to intervene militarily in Central America after 1920 it has, in the long run, worsened the situation it meant to correct....*"[50]

While American political tendencies within the Reagan White House molded US policy toward El Salvador, only the nature of the Salvadoran state could serve to define the success or failure of that policy. In other words, the American president could not directly influence the people of El Salvador; instead, his chosen method of engagement would affect the people of El Salvador only after interaction with and through the Salvadoran context. As in any other case, this context involves an expansive array of variables including the history and demographics as well as other characteristics distinct to the region, the state and its dealings with other entities. Most of these considerations are beyond the scope of this paper, but three are relevant in that they acted to disrupt US-Salvadoran interaction specifically during the years of the first Reagan Administration.

---

[50] Leiken, Robert S., ed. *Central America: Anatomy of Conflict.* (New York: Pergamon Press, 1984), 64.

El Salvador: The Strongman Mentality and Lack of Democratic Institutions

The history of El Salvador thrust upon its people a cultural context that created real expectations for how a state should operate. Perhaps penultimate in their minds was the utility of a strong central government. Rather than insisting on a government that operated in the interests of all its citizens, cultural influences led the people to believe that a single man – a strongman – should function as the sole arbiter of power in the state. Inevitably, this man would arrive via the corridors of the military,[51] so he could wield and maintain the power required of one who led through directives and not electoral mandates.

Indeed, elections were and continue to be peripheral to politics in Central America.[52] Whereas the distinctive American experience had borne out the utility of elections as a means by which political power could stably transfer from one leader to the next, the same cannot be said for Central American states like El Salvador; indeed, if anything, the history of the Salvadoran state demonstrated government functions were best exercised within the confines of an semi-authoritarian regime. Reagan's first-term attempts at promoting the American electoral construct within El Salvador revealed either that he did not appreciate the lack of coherent historical precedent elections held in Central American politics or he could not compensate for that knowledge through policy. Time and again, Reagan and his administration proponents referred to elections in general as the only true harbinger of democracy[53] and "a practical yardstick of democracy," even though that 'yardstick' often proved to be fraught with fraudulent activity

---

[51] Max G. Manwaring and Court Prisk, *El Salvador at War: An Oral History of Conflict from the 1979 Insurrection to the Present* (Washington, D.C.: National Defense University Press, 1988), 118.

[52] Walter LaFeber, *Inevitable Revolutions: The United States in Central America.* exp. ed. (New York: W.W. Norton, 1984), 287.

[53] Ibid., 249.

within the Salvadoran state.[54] Instead of 'spanning the gap' between cultures within a framework

that both nations could grasp, the American administration demurred and simply expected the

advantages of election-based democracy to become self-evident to the Salvadoran people. That

faulty expectation combined with military-centric policy initiatives actually contributed to a

reversal of fortune of sorts: the military strongman mentality became even more ingrained in the

Salvadoran consciousness. As Johnson said, "The injection of a large U.S. military presence in

Honduras, the heavy involvement of Honduras and El Salvador in the contra war in Nicaragua,

and the large increases in U.S. military assistance to countries of the region have strengthened the

hand of the military within these societies."[55]

The historical preeminence of the military was not the only reason why democratic

institutions failed to mature within El Salvador. Structural obstacles existed as well, highlighted

by those associated with the economy and the military. As an agrarian state, the nation developed

governmental institutions to the extent they were needed to exploit the land and coordinate the

exportation of goods.[56] Unlike other countries with a history of democracy, Salvadoran

institutions were not strong enough to serve as protectorates for liberal thought during times of

political transition; according to Ambassador Thomas Pickering, this opinion was reflected down

as far as the rural populations who knew and expected nothing other than authoritarianism.[57]

---

[54] Ibid., 311. Note: Contemporary thinking accepts that not until his second administration did Reagan privately embraced democracy as a primary goal for El Salvador. Nonetheless, his first-term administration used language and proposed initiatives that implied he was a proponent of Salvadoran democracy from the outset of his tenure in the White House.

[55] Robert H. Johnson, "Misguided Morality: Ethics and the Reagan Doctrine." *Political Science Quarterly* 103, no. 3 (Autumn 1988): 526.

[56] Max G. Manwaring and Court Prisk, *El Salvador at War: An Oral History of Conflict from the 1979 Insurrection to the Present* (Washington, D.C.: National Defense University Press, 1988), 6.

[57] Ibid., 10.

This acceptance of authoritarianism extended well beyond the civilian population. Militarily, General Wallace Nutting, Commander in Chief, Southern Command (CINCSOUTH, the combatant commander responsible for Central America), cited mounting evidence from advisory groups that a sharp divide existed between the Salvadoran officer and the enlisted personnel.[58] The former group was meant to command with no input or feedback from the latter. This schism in the army reflected the same attitudes within Salvadoran society as a whole, pitting the privileged against the commoner. Similar to a caste system, Salvadoran society more accurately might have been described as a composition of several communities with disparate agendas rather than one entity befitting the term 'nation.' Viewed in this light, the lack of democratic institutions and the apparent societal need for a strong leader then comes as no surprise.

United States: Lack of a Long-Term Engagement Plan

The strategic impulses that led the Reagan administration to misinterpret Salvadoran political expectations actually had a much broader impact. In particular, Reagan proved unable shirk his ideological preconceptions, leading to his inability to distinguish not only internal Salvadoran dynamics, but also the overall framework of the conflict itself. Ideological leanings were perhaps most evident when airing its opinion of Central American politics. Few other reasons can describe the president's view that issues confronting Central America resulted from "a Soviet-Cuban power play—pure and simple."[59] This overly simplistic view communicated a level of certitude that was consistent with the "know how to help" ideology that drove administration policy. And, given the times – the Soviet Union was still nearly a decade away

---

[58] Ibid., 102.

26

from collapse – his position appears to be rational. The relevant critique of this position, however, is that the attitude conveyed did not welcome the introduction of counterfactual information. The resulting lack of intellectual curiosity at best delayed and at worst prevented policy from maturing as situational understanding improved.

The failure to understand the developing Salvadoran dynamic – whether conscious or unconscious in its origin – afflicted most levels of the administration. The two key institutions responsible for the application of US policy in the region, the State Department and the Department of Defense, spent much of the early 1980s in an ongoing dispute over everything from problem framing to the appropriate employment of solutions.[60] As evidence of their at-times public disagreement, a Pentagon source was once quoted as cynically asking the State Department: "Tell us whether the problem (in Central America) is one of social and internal upheaval or Communist-inspired subversion: whether the problem is military or broader and deeper and much more intractable."[61]

Guidance from the Oval Office did not prove to be any more enlightening. Critics charged that after nearly a year in office, Reagan himself "had failed to explain his foreign policies" making it "difficult to find evidence that a design had been constructed which connected policy and tactics."[62] Even when guidance was given, it failed to convey any sense of true direction. Ambassador Hinton claimed that his marching orders from the president were limited

---

[59] Robert A. Pastor, "Explaining U.S. Policy Toward the Caribbean Basin: Fixed and Emerging Images." *World Politics* 38, no. 3 (Apr. 1986): 488.

[60] Walter LaFeber, *Inevitable Revolutions: The United States in Central America.* exp. ed. (New York: W.W. Norton, 1984), 276.

[61] Laurence Whitehead. "Explaining Washington's Central American Policies," *Journal of Latin American Studies* 15, no. 2 (Nov. 1983): 346.

[62] Enrique A. Baloyra, "Central America on the Reagan Watch: Rhetoric and Reality." *Journal of Interamerican Studies and World Affairs* 27, no. 1 (Feb. 1985): 38. Note: This omission of policy was

to undertaking such action that would help prevent the communist takeover of the Salvadoran state.[63] Although that did offer him wide-ranging latitude to deal with the situation as he saw fit, that guidance generally convinced the Ambassador that the Oval Office did not retain an enthusiastic inclination for feedback. Whether this was the president's intention or not may merit discussion, but it in any case is another example of how his ideological certainty shaped his direction to subordinates. And even to the extent Reagan appeared to allow policy drift, his key advisors did little to smooth the waters.

Other key administration officials also contributed to policy imprecision: United Nations Ambassador Jeanne Kirkpatrick attempted to define a fine – some might say nonexistent – line between "good" authoritarian and "bad" totalitarian leaders in an attempt to justify Reagan policies in Central America and elsewhere. Her effort drew outrage from a variety of sources across the ideological spectrum and exacerbated the level of policy paralysis within the Reagan White House.[64] Meanwhile Secretary of State Haig, like Kirkpatrick a principal who spoke with the president's implicit approval,[65] inadvertently continued to ensure discord at the policymaking level. During his relatively short tenure, Secretary Haig argued the Salvadoran conflict provided communism a point of entry into the region, a communication wholly in line with the president's

---

later revealed to be a conscious decision on the president's part, but nonetheless contributed to significant policy drift within his administration.

[63] Max G. Manwaring and Court Prisk, *El Salvador at War: An Oral History of Conflict from the 1979 Insurrection to the Present* (Washington, D.C.: National Defense University Press, 1988), 111.

[64] Walter LaFeber, *Inevitable Revolutions: The United States in Central America.* exp. ed. (New York: W.W. Norton, 1984), 278-279.

[65] Note: Several sources, including Baloyra, ("Central America on the Reagan Watch: Rhetoric and Reality"), have since indicated that Haig did not enjoy Reagan's full confidence or the confidence of his other key advisors. This, however, immediately raises the question why Haig remained as Secretary of State – perhaps the key foreign policy position in US government – for the first half of Reagan's first term. His continued presence indicates either presidential approval of his actions or a willingness on the part of the president to accept an actor in that role who might issue contravening guidance rather than face the political repercussions of having to replace his Secretary of State so early in his administration.

anti-communist stance and emerging doctrine.[66] At the same time, however, he at one time

claimed the American nuns who were gunned down in cold blood in El Salvador, reputedly by

right-wing death squads, were actually shot trying to run a roadblock – an outrageous assertion.[67]

The irony is clear: Reagan's principal diplomatic agent – the man in charge of implementing

administration foreign policy – could not discern even the most obvious of Salvadoran battle

lines. Ensuing guidance from the office of the Secretary of State was most likely treated

accordingly by State subordinates, leaving the US foreign policy 'ship' adrift without a rudder.

Comprehension of the Salvadoran problem was marginally better in the military realm.

General Nutting was one of the first to identify the overall lack of campaign plan for the United

States in its Salvadoran effort.[68] With his encouragement and the approval from then-

Ambassador Hinton, a commission led by Brigadier General Frederick Woerner submitted a

report recognizing this shortfall, recommending a way ahead for administration policy in El

Salvador. Its contribution to the Salvadoran military strategy notwithstanding, the commission's

report emphasized the limited utility of military aid in resolving the conflict; by clashing with the

military-centric Reagan Doctrine, however, it fell on deaf ears within administration circles.[69] If

nothing else, had the administration given the Woerner Commission its due, the report could have

contributed substantially to reducing the level of policy discord that developed between the

administration, its agents and the military commanders responsible for the region. As Senator

Christopher Dodd, an admitted administration critic, claimed in 1983, "there is total confusion in

---

[66] Walter LaFeber, *Inevitable Revolutions: The United States in Central America.* exp. ed. (New York: W.W. Norton, 1984), 274.

[67] Robert D. Schulzinger, "Foreign Policy." *American Quarterly* 35, no. 1/2, Special Issue: Contemporary America (Spring - Summer 1983): 57.

[68] Max G. Manwaring and Court Prisk, *El Salvador at War: An Oral History of Conflict from the 1979 Insurrection to the Present* (Washington, D.C.: National Defense University Press, 1988), 222-229.

[69] Note: Congress did give the report some credence

Washington as to what the administration's policies are, and there is a total confusion in Central America as to what U.S. intentions are."[70]

US-Salvadoran Dissonance

As Senator Dodd's comment and the brief history described above shows, dissonance was not new to the relationship between the United States and the Central American countries. Dealings during Reagan's first term were no exception. Although both administration officials and their Salvadoran counterparts share the blame for what resulted from a lack of effective communication, the Reagan administration may be guilty of creating the barriers to success in the first place. After all, it was the administration's overly simplistic view of the revolutionaries in El Salvador which prohibited them from achieving an accurate measure of the revolutionaries' true intentions.[71] Indeed, as a Boston Globe editorial said in reference to the Salvadoran conflict and others in the region, "It is simple enough to call that communism or totalitarianism and support the people who shoot to kill it, but it ignores the fact that no amount of foreign-supported military might can suppress indefinitely a people who are more driven by want than by ideology.[72] In the end, discordant beliefs and assumptions about each other and the enemy disrupted the US-Salvadoran relationship that it often seemed as if they were fighting two different wars.

This discord took place on several levels, from the highest policymakers to the American liaison groups in the Salvadoran military. Most of the confusion emanated from the executive level between President Jose Napoleon Duarte and President Reagan's inner circle and sprung

---

[70] Mary Vanderlaan, "The Dual Strategy Myth in Central American Policy." *Journal of Interamerican Studies and World Affairs* 26, no. 2 (May 1984): 199.

[71] Walter LaFeber, *Inevitable Revolutions: The United States in Central America.* exp. ed. (New York: W.W. Norton, 1984), 275-276.

[72] "Oligarchy of Terrorism," *Boston Globe,* May 25, 1981.

from a lack of coherent strategy on the part of the American administration. Clarity did not

improve in lower echelons:

> Asked to characterize U.S. objectives in the war, he (a senior US military officer) answered (as paraphrased by the authors) that the White House was hoping for "a bright shiny democracy to spring into being overnight," that the State Department was preoccupied with surviving the next vote on capitol Hill, the Defense Department worried lest controversy over El Salvador jeopardize other defense programs, the Congress strove to prevent El Salvador from becoming another Vietnam, the Central Intelligence Agency was absorbed in attempting to manipulate Salvadoran political factions, while SOUTHCOM [U.S. military command of the war effort, based in Panama] searched for ways to "let the government of El Salvador operate without too much fear of interference from the insurgents."[73]

Misunderstandings were particularly evident to all observers at the Ambassadorial and Theater

Commander level.

Even if situational understanding was better at the level of policy execution – the military

equivalent of the operational or tactical level of war – dissonance was such that true measures of

success were often difficult to identify, much less achieve. Ambassador Hinton saw this

firsthand: as the point man for policy in country, he often viewed the US and Salvadoran

militaries at odds with who was in charge. According to him, CINCSOUTH attempted to assume

responsibility for the war and coordinate it from his headquarters in Panama while the

Salvadorans saw the civil war as a problem of their own.[74] This disagreement highlights the

cognitive abyss between the two nations. Whereas the American military commander felt it his

duty to ensure US military aid was utilized appropriately (a response appropriate from the

American standpoint), the Salvadorans rightfully may have seen American 'responsibility' for the

war as an affront to their Latin heritage or *machismo*. Aside from the purely cultural

---

[73] William Bollinger, "Villalobos on "Popular Insurrection"." *Latin American Perspectives* 16, no. 3, Revolutionary Strategy in Central America (Summer 1989): 40.

[74] Max G. Manwaring and Court Prisk, *El Salvador at War: An Oral History of Conflict from the 1979 Insurrection to the Present* (Washington, D.C.: National Defense University Press, 1988), 104-105.

implications, the insult was even more striking in that it occurred in a nation that rarely, if ever, questioned the supremacy of its own military.

In addition to external challenges from the Americans, the Salvadoran military found its own *raison d'être* challenged by the insurgents. Not surprisingly, leftist leaders viewed the Salvadoran military as a puppet for the United States.[75] On the surface, it may have appeared they were, what with the enormous amount of military aid Reagan funneled into the country in the early part of the decade. Given the aforementioned friction between the two countries militaries, however, that conclusion might be interpreted as too shallow. The truth lies somewhere in the middle, but the guerrillas position may have been more accurate than one might otherwise imagine: one of President Duarte's key, if then private, complaints about the Reagan administration involved the unilateral decision by Washington to integrate military advisors into Salvadoran units, a move made without his consultation.[76] Ostensibly working for the civil-military junta under Duarte's leadership, the advisor issue is just one way in which the military 'worked' for the American government.

The advisor issue also serves as an example of dissonance at the tactical level of operations. Advisors were deemed necessary since Reagan officials had been unimpressed by the professionalism of the Salvadoran military.[77] Harkening back to the Vietnam years, policymakers decided the best way to coordinate efforts (and ensure Salvadoran compliance with what they saw as a US-led effort) was to insert military advisors into the field. Those officers should have brought greater clarity to US understanding of the obstacles in El Salvador, but since

---

[75] Ibid., 110.

[76] Ibid., 112.

[77] Walter LaFeber, *Inevitable Revolutions: The United States in Central America.* exp. ed. (New York: W.W. Norton, 1984), 284.

other substantive comments did not resonate with the Reagan administrations understanding of the problem, it is hard to imagine how they would have had any impact on strategic decisions either.

Despite its lack of confidence in the Salvadoran military, the White House's critical lack of knowledge in the Central American region as a whole[78] led them to underestimate the power of the revolutionaries to the degree that it outweighed any need to upgrade Salvadoran military training, or so administration officials thought. The strength of the guerrilla uprisings of 1983 caught administration officials off guard and a "crash course" of American-style officer training in El Salvador ensued.[79] American advisors recognized that Salvadoran officer training was fundamental to the transformation of the Salvadoran military. That training would allow the military to absorb and utilize the massive amounts of US military assistance proffered by the administration. Nonetheless, it took a full three years for the American strategic leadership to acknowledge this same need.

Influences Meet Obstacles: Interaction within El Salvador

Lack of a Viable Political Actor

A significant obstacle to achieving US policy goals in El Salvador was the lack of a reputable national government. Though the need to establish legitimate control at the national level was implicitly understood,[80] finding an actor to do Washington's bidding proved difficult.

---

[78] Ibid., 277.

[79] Max G. Manwaring and Court Prisk, *El Salvador at War: An Oral History of Conflict from the 1979 Insurrection to the Present* (Washington, D.C.: National Defense University Press, 1988), 165.

[80] Leiken, Robert S., ed. *Central America: Anatomy of Conflict.* (New York: Pergamon Press, 1984), 64-65.

During Reagan's first term, only two governments offered an alternative to the guerilla-inspired communist model and demonstrated any empirical chance of success: the traditional government supported by the oligarchy, and the coalition government, anchored by a mixture of centrist parties. By the early 1980s, the traditional government had begun to break free from the oligarchy, but was still subject to claims of obligation to the whims of the violent right wing, making it a poor choice for any American support. In the end, the coalition government model was the only one the American president could legitimately support, but its ability to coalesce national power under its oversight drew criticism from the start.

As previously alluded, the key player in domestic Salvadoran politics during this time proved to be Jose Napoleon Duarte. An erstwhile reformer and ex-Mayor of San Salvador, he participated in the civil-military junta that governed El Salvador in the early 1980s. His inclusion in the ruling junta made sense: Duarte's reformist tendencies were certain to generate an air of credibility in the eyes of the Americans, but the collaborative nature of the junta limited his ability to exercise power independent of the military.[81]

As the one true institution with power in El Salvador, the military may well have been attracted to increased American engagement under Reagan since his approach would coincidentally serve domestic military interests. Specifically, the Reagan Doctrine would play into the hands of the military by augmenting its resources and ensuring its continued control of civil El Salvador while also girding its units for the fight against the communists. Placing Duarte the reformer as the public face of the Salvadoran government may have served as the 'grease' to ensure continued American involvement. So the Reagan Doctrine, itself a natural outflow of the doctrinal and ideological influences affecting the president, found an eager test case in the form

---

[81] Walter LaFeber, *Inevitable Revolutions: The United States in Central America.* exp. ed. (New York: W.W. Norton, 1984), 250.

of the Salvadoran military. But this confluence of interests would do nothing if not ensure the

continued cycle of oppressive state control that had led El Salvador to crisis in the first place.

Robert Johnson cited the Reagan Doctrine as one of the key reasons why

> the fragile democracies of the area depend very heavily upon the sufferance of the
> military for survival. As one writer has put it, "The struggle faced by Central America's
> elected presidents is . . . to broaden the civilian authority as far as possible without
> exceeding the limits set by the military's idea of its own welfare."[82]

While certainly not the only reason why civilian control of the Salvadoran government relied

upon military support, the Reagan Doctrine did nothing if not further the sense that military

preeminence in Salvadoran life was normal and acceptable.

From the outset, Duarte felt his perception of what was normal and acceptable in

Salvadoran life neatly dovetailed with Reagan administration goals. Reagan's advisors, however,

were more concerned with his motives. According to Duarte himself, Reagan's inner circle

seemed to be coached by the Salvadoran right to disbelieve his Christian Democratic Party's

dedication to reinvigorating private enterprise in El Salvador. His worry only increased after

Reagan's principals "interrogated" him about his thoughts on agrarian reform.[83] The reasons for

this continuing doubt in Duarte – someone official administration policy had openly and actively

promoted[84] – are unclear, but it may have been because administration officials saw the right-

wing military, as chief recipients of aid from the US, and not the centrists as the means by which

they could ultimately achieve a non-communist government in El Salvador; alternatively, and

perhaps more likely, it could have been an acknowledgement by the administration that they

---

[82] Robert H. Johnson, "Misguided Morality: Ethics and the Reagan Doctrine." *Political Science Quarterly* 103, no. 3 (Autumn 1988): 526.

[83] Max G. Manwaring and Court Prisk, *El Salvador at War: An Oral History of Conflict from the 1979 Insurrection to the Present* (Washington, D.C.: National Defense University Press, 1988), 99-100.

[84] Jorge Nef, "The Trend Toward Democratization and Redemocratization in Latin America: Shadow and Substance." *Latin American Research Review* 23, no. 3 (1988): 136.

viewed Duarte's presidency as a 'blip' of history, unlikely to serve as the catalyst for a democratic tradition within El Salvador despite the vigor with which it publicly supported his party.[85] Interestingly enough, in light of their initial reservations about Duarte, the Reagan administration found no other ready alternative within El Salvador.

Duarte's first real political test nearly proved to be his last. The Constituent Elections of 1982 tested not only Duarte's legitimacy as a political leader, but also his role as the de facto agent for American-style democracy in El Salvador. Widely expected *by the Americans* to win the election, Duarte's Christian Democratic party lost to the right-wing (and death-squad affiliated) Nationalist Republican Alliance (ARENA). [86] Wilbur Landrey comments that this should not have been a surprise:

> The administration kept claiming that Christian Democratic President Jose Napoleon Duarte was making progress. He may have made some, but hobbled as he was by the power of the Salvadoran army and alleged corruption, it was too little and came too late.
>
> Salvadorans responded with what was regarded as more of a ``punishment vote`` against Duarte than support for the ultra-right Nationalist Republican Alliance (ARENA).[87]

It is presumptive to assume that punishment was meant for the United States, but since the 1982 protest vote was directed toward the American's anointed agent in El Salvador, the US image could not have emerged unscathed.

In truth, fraud was widely viewed to be a problem during the election and this may have changed the outcome of the vote. Nonetheless, this experience should have served as a clear indicator to the administration that its foreign policy was adrift. In the two years since implementation, Reagan policy had neither achieved the explicit goal of ensuring Duarte's

---

[85] Ibid., 137.

[86] Walter LaFeber, *Inevitable Revolutions: The United States in Central America.* exp. ed. (New York: W.W. Norton, 1984), 251.

[87] Wilbur G. Landrey, "A Shambles in Central America," *St.Petersburg Times,* March 31 1988.

political survivability nor the implicit goal of creating a democratic state through the electoral process. Undeterred and apparently unconscious to the lesson at hand, the administration claimed the vote a victory for democracy, even if it was a failure for Duarte.

The success of the centrist government formed by the 1984 elections and led by Duarte was similarly doomed from the start.[88] Condemned by his problematic history associated with his loss in the 1972 elections and subsequent exile,[89] and his party's embarrassing loss in the 1982 elections, Duarte found himself the public champion of a model of government unproven at the Salvadoran national level during modern times. So even though the military's grip over the Salvadoran government had ebbed by 1984, the country and its citizens were still ill-prepared to assume and quite skeptical of any move to openly embrace a moderate democratic model, much less one based on American tenants. For its part, the Oval Office was unable to convince them otherwise.

As late as 1984, the President himself attempted to validate the presence of moderating forces within El Salvador by stating in a speech that support for the Central American country did not require a choice between extremes.[90] Since his point was brokered in truth the fact he made such a sweeping statement is not the point; that he made no mention of whether any of the non-

---

[88] Kenneth E. Sharpe, "The Post-Vietnam Formula Under Siege: The Imperial Presidency and Central America." *Political Science Quarterly* 102, no. 4 (Winter 1987): 557.

[89] Max G. Manwaring and Court Prisk, *El Salvador at War: An Oral History of Conflict from the 1979 Insurrection to the Present* (Washington, D.C.: National Defense University Press, 1988), 13. Note: Duarte participated in a coup after the army interfered with the 1972 presidential elections (elections he would have legitimately won had the army not intervened). The collapse of the coup drove him into exile for the next several years.

[90] "Transcript of President's Speech on Central America Policy," *New York Times,* May 10 1984. Note: Reagan's exact words follow: "Some argue that El Salvador has only political extremes - the violent left and the violent right – and that we must choose between them. That is just not true. Democratic political parties range from the democratic left to center to conservative." He makes no further comment qualifying these remarks.

extremist groups were politically viable is, however, notable. Reagan's implication aside, no centrist model held any significant sway over the Salvadoran people during most of 1980s independent of military support.

In fact, the whole concept of representative government within El Salvador was viewed with doubt. Guillermo Ungo, a guerilla leader within El Salvador believed that "governments of El Salvador have long kept in place unjust institutions and policies that have excluded the majority of the people from real participation...."[91] Far from an objective analysis, to be sure, but Ungo's sentiments rang true with most of the Salvadoran population. Elizabeth Wood was more specific and yet much less gracious when she depicted the Salvadoran government as consisting of "coalitions of economic elites and military hardliners [defending] labor-repressive institutions and practices until the civil war."[92]

Those coalitions and repressive institutions succeeded in holding Duarte's reforms at bay. As indicated, while Duarte demonstrated the best of intentions in El Salvador, his impotence was due largely to considerations well beyond his span of control (although the degree to which he could control corruption within his party is arguable). His attempts to garner support via elections were truly weakened by the overall lack of democratic institutions. The strongman tendencies described previously were inconsistent with long-term, stable democratic institutions. Reagan's incomplete strategy in El Salvador did nothing to improve things, as they simply promoted a system whereby elections identified a leader, but did not distribute power. As a half-hearted measure lacking the comprehensiveness necessary to ensure power transition, American-

---

[91] Ibid., 7.

[92] Elisabeth Jean Wood, *Forging Democracy from Below.* (Cambridge: Cambridge University Press, 2000), 25.

supported elections gave the population no reason to expect anyone other than a figurehead would serve as president in a Salvadoran democracy.

And though tainted by complaints of corruption, Duarte did shirk much of the 'figurehead' moniker in the years prior to his death in 1990, providing him some political space to initiate peace negotiations with the rebels.[93] By the time he could exercise power independent of the army, he was undermined by the reluctance of the very people he tried to assist. At the time, the citizens of El Salvador did not know, understand or trust the democracy Duarte offered. In truth, then, it seems Reagan's military-centric approach may have inadvertently inhibited Duarte's rise to legitimacy in the eyes of the Salvadoran people by prolonging the military's centralized control of the state.

The 'Supply Side' Approach

President Reagan's new policy was not limited to calls for political change. He also attempted to bolster the country's economic system by requesting a large increase in overall aid for the country as well. A major part of the package involved dramatically increasing the military aid to the Salvadoran military in the hopes that they could quickly win the war. However, just as the administration had misread (albeit not entirely) the intentions of the revolutionaries, it also made mistakes in seeking solutions to the Salvadoran problem. Reagan administration solutions to the Salvadoran problem might well be described in the jargon of his well-known economic plan: a supply-side approach.

---

[93] Baloyra, Enrique A. "Negotiating War in El Salvador: The Politics of Endgame." *Journal of Interamerican Studies and World Affairs* 28, no. 1 (Spring 1986): 123.

The supply-side approach had two major facets. One, administration officials felt that the revolution in El Salvador could be starved to death by interdicting its manpower and supply lines, in theory emanating from outside the state. Though this may have worked, their approach was faulty from the start because the revolution did not rely entirely on outside supply lines as they expected; instead, indigenous support proved to be the key to the revolutionaries' strength.[94] This is not to say the supply-side approach did not work: Colonel Carlos Reynauldo Lopez Nuila, Vice-Minister of Public Security for El Salvador, confirmed cutting off supplies could and did adversely affect guerrillas in their sanctuaries.[95] However, these sanctuaries fell outside the borders of El Salvador and the administration mistakenly believed that starving external sanctuaries of support would have a domino effect downstream, inevitably collapsing rebel bases within El Salvador. Continued rebel activities proved American policymakers wrong. The misled perception that the revolt could be starved of supplies convinced the administration it could hold fast to the second principle governing its activities in El Salvador: the policy of no negotiations.

In a country that retained no institutional mechanism for redressing grievances,[96] negotiations seemed to be the one way where violence could be addressed successfully. As Landrey said, "A priority for the next president should be a policy toward Central America in which anti-communism does not blot out recognition of the poverty and injustice responsible for

---

[94] Jerome Slater, "Dominos in Central America: Will they Fall? Does it Matter?" *International Security* 12, no. 2 (Autumn 1987): 108.

[95] Max G. Manwaring and Court Prisk, *El Salvador at War: An Oral History of Conflict from the 1979 Insurrection to the Present* (Washington, D.C.: National Defense University Press, 1988), 161.

[96] Ibid., 84.

its problems."[97] Occasions to achieve dialogue posed themselves to the Reagan administration at multiple times, but each time policymakers failed to seize the opportunity.

The Carter-to-Reagan transition in the winter of 1980 actually created the first windows of opportunity for peace in El Salvador under Reagan's watch. Specifically, the perceived differences in attitude between the two administrations created waves within the guerrilla movement. Reagan's desire to offer the Salvadoran government relatively unqualified support was so transparent to the guerrillas that the FMLN decided on an ill-conceived "Final Offensive" in January 1981. Their goal was to end the war before the expected influx of American military support could be brought to bear on the side of the government, potentially swaying the tide of the war.[98]

Their ensuing failure led many in the guerrilla movement to seek dialogue with the Reagan administration, but the president refused such overtures.[99] Granted, not all guerrillas were inclined to make peace – many fought since they believed only violence would bring about the revolution they sought – but in this case the rebels were rejected outright, with little or no preliminary interchange among even the most junior of intermediaries.[100]. A similar scenario occurred as the 1982 Constituent Assembly elections approached. With the Salvadoran government offering to place leftist candidates on the ballot in exchange for a decrease in

---

[97] Wilbur G. Landrey, "A Shambles in Central America," *St.Petersburg Times,* March 31, 1988.

[98] Brian J. Bosch, *The Salvadoran Officer Corps and the Final Offensive of 1981.* (Jefferson, NC: McFarland, 1999),75.

[99]Max G. Manwaring and Court Prisk, *El Salvador at War: An Oral History of Conflict from the 1979 Insurrection to the Present* (Washington, D.C.: National Defense University Press, 1988), 109

[100] Walter LaFeber, *Inevitable Revolutions: The United States in Central America.* exp. ed. (New York: W.W. Norton, 1984), 286.

violence, guerilla forces instead approached the US directly for talks "without any preconditions by any of the parties to the conflict." A quick American rejection followed.[101]

Colonel James Steele, the military group commander in El Salvador at the time, related how a third scenario came to pass after Duarte's election in 1984: leftist guerillas suffered tremendous attrition[102] and approached the US about negotiating a peace; again, they were rebuffed. In all three instances, spanning the entire breadth of the first Reagan administration, the rejection of rebel rapprochement conveyed an outright adherence to Reagan's staunch anti-communist precepts (and a corresponding confidence in their ultimate success), a failed grasp of the variables at play, or, most likely, elements of both.

The president's approach stood in stark contrast to some of his key military advisors on the issue. When asked about the State Department's proposal to cut off the international supply lines to the revolutionaries, General Nutting "warned that past efforts to cut off supply routes, in Italy during World War II, for example, had not been very successful."[103] His comments were substantiated by the 1983 Woerner Commission report cited earlier. But even credible criticisms like these were insufficient to sway opinion at the presidential level; the policy ship, as it were, had already left port and midcourse corrections would not come until after Reagan's second inauguration.

---

[101] Ibid. Note: One reason the guerillas eventually chose to ignore the Salvadoran overtures for peace prior to the 1982 elections was the government's inability to provide protection for any candidate publicly supporting the leftist agenda. The months leading up the elections saw widespread circulation of a list of rebels to be shot on sight.

[102] Max G. Manwaring and Court Prisk, *El Salvador at War: An Oral History of Conflict from the 1979 Insurrection to the Present* (Washington, D.C.: National Defense University Press, 1988), 146.

[103] Laurence Whitehead. "Explaining Washington's Central American Policies," *Journal of Latin American Studies* 15, no. 2 (Nov. 1983): 346.

Conclusion

Reagan's first-term policies were designed to accomplish one key task: the establishment of a stable, non-communist and ostensibly democratic regime in El Salvador. His first-term administration's Salvadoran policy approach failed for a variety of reasons. Instead of achieving his vision, his policies at best failed to address pre-existent cultural influences within the Salvadoran state, resulting in mediocre policy. At worst, his approach magnified those influences within the state and probably delayed the arrival of a peaceful resolution to the civil war. No matter the historical impact of his administration, Reagan's first term actions toward El Salvador provided a wealth of learning points for his approach there.

These observations only become evident after viewing Reagan's first term approaches to Salvadoran policy through a bridging analysis. The two other methods of examination, American- and Salvadoran-centric, tell but one side of the story and fail to yield generalized observations useful for future study. Instead, they tend to attribute cause-and-effect based on faulty assumptions. Whereas the Reagan administration had every reason to expect their policy course in El Salvador would succeed, their beliefs were based on a flawed and incomplete picture of the contextual elements within Salvadoran society. The domestic influences that encouraged (and very nearly demanded) American involvement in El Salvador also played a key role in ensuring policy failure.

As has been shown, domestic influences played a central role in the formulation of American foreign policy. The evolution of doctrinal influences since the Monroe Doctrine encouraged intervention into El Salvador; Reagan's ideological position appeared to provide a ready solution to the problem, in effect achieving the political equivalent of serendipity. Unfortunately, the translation of domestic influences into practical policy belied the complexity of the situation in El Salvador and contributed only to unsuitable outcomes. While the doctrinal influences relied predominantly upon historical precedent, ideological premises were a sole construct of the president and his staff. Therein lays the first observation.

The incorporation of ideology as a way to frame a problem is understandable, reasonable and expected; the relevant lesson this case offers has to with how to employ ideology. As a starting point, ideology provides a basis for common understanding – a way to thematically interpret world events. But in the end, it is better suited as a point of departure for intellectual curiosity than a destination. Those who use ideology as the framework for policy are obliged to define the parameters within which they see acceptable outcomes. It appears that in this case Reagan's first administration condensed his position to allow for only two outcomes (either a communist or a noncommunist government) – as if to convey the importance of Salvadoran initiatives relative to others[104] – and communicated it through the use of Cold War metaphors. In reality, a multitude of end states existed. A particular example of this can be found in the manner in which the Reagan administration repeatedly denied the leftists even a minimal stake in the Salvadoran government out of fear of an 'inevitable' communist takeover.

Intense ideological foundations also drove the president to ignore pragmatic approaches that tested the validity of policy assumptions at each stage. Although the argument may be made that pragmatism often evolves into relativism and is therefore an unwelcome approach, the implementation of presidential policy still demanded some sort of feedback mechanism. Administration officials should have seen the need for some alternative method for discovering the so-called 'ground truth' information from policy implementers. Instead, evidence indicates the administration wielded its ideology like a sword, threatening to cut off anyone who dared counter the administration position. Uncontrolled ideologically-based approaches to policy confine decision makers to rational objectives that are too often predetermined and inflexible to contravening information.

_____

[104] For more on this tendency, see Robert D. Schulzinger "Foreign Policy." *American Quarterly* 35, no. 1/2, Special Issue: Contemporary America (Spring - Summer 1983): 39.

In Reagan's defense and from a strictly American standpoint, his policy approach appeared rational and should have worked. But defending an initiative based on its rationality bears fruit only if that rationality also resonates with the policy's target audience (in this case, the Salvadorans). A basic lack of understanding and oversimplification of the Salvadoran problem ensured Reagan policies would fail the Salvadoran rationality test. Furthermore, by introducing foreign concepts (like American-style democracy) to Salvadoran society, his administration was placed in the unenviable position of defending changes that offered the average citizen few immediate advantages over their current system. Administration proponents could never answer the most telling question asked by Salvadorans when viewing reforms within their country: "What's in it for me?"[105]

The inability to answer that question highlights this case's third lesson: the hazards associated with abrupt formulation of strategy. Since doctrinal and ideological influences provided a 'ready' solution to the Salvadoran problem, strategy formulation suffered; few, if any, at any level fully understood the administration's plan for success. Most importantly, given the role the military played in implementation of policy, commanders within that chain of command found themselves unsure of their role, their responsibilities, and even in some cases, their desired end state.

In and of itself, however, this did not signify the death knell for Salvadoran policy during the first Reagan administration. As in this case, improper strategies can be overcome, but doing so requires the escalation of involvement by the foreign actor in the inner workings of the state (something few parties desired). The new strategy must overcome not only the obstacles that hampered the first failed strategy, but also the previous strategy itself since it, too, contributes to

---

[105] Max G. Manwaring and Court Prisk, *El Salvador at War: An Oral History of Conflict from the 1979 Insurrection to the Present* (Washington, D.C.: National Defense University Press, 1988), 6.

an increased inertia within the system. This clearly did not happen. Inasmuch as the American strategy remained incomplete, it could not provide Salvadorans any tangible inducement to support change.

Finally, this case speaks to the value of understanding the implications of vast cultural chasms between societies. Cultural influences exercise particular relevance during civil wars since those experiences are common in some form or another to each participant. This was particularly the case in El Salvador, where oftentimes the only uninformed participant was the strategic leadership of the United States. Whereas Reagan's attempts to solve the Salvadoran problem may have worked in a country that mirrored American social, political and economic overtones, they were bound to fail unless molded to specifically address the issues facing a country with El Salvador's distinct history. Most significantly, Reagan policy initiatives, incomplete as they were, seemed at times designed to satisfy his administration's needs – validating those 'we need to act' and 'we know how to help' influences – than they were to satisfy the needs of the Salvadoran state. In this way, American policy influences and Salvadoran cultural influences conspired to restrict any measurable success in El Salvador during Reagan's first term.

BIBLIOGRAPHY

Agee, Philip, and Warner Poelchau. *White Paper Whitewash: Interviews with Philip Agee on the CIA and El Salvador.* New York: Deep Cover Books, 1981.

Albiac, María Dolores. "Perdón Sin Olvido: El Perdón Del Presidente Salvadoreño Alfredo Cristiani Dejará Libres a Los Acusados De Atrocidades De Guerra." *Cambio 16* (March 29, 1993): 82-84.

Bacevich, A. J. *American Military Policy in Small Wars : The Case of El Salvador.* Cambridge, Mass.; Washington: Institute for Foreign Policy Analysis; Pergamon-Brassey's International Defense Publishers, 1988.

Baloyra, Enrique A. "Negotiating War in El Salvador: The Politics of Endgame." *Journal of Interamerican Studies and World Affairs* 28, no. 1 (Spring 1986): 123-147.

------. "Central America on the Reagan Watch: Rhetoric and Reality." *Journal of Interamerican Studies and World Affairs* 27, no. 1 (Feb. 1985): 35-62.

------. *El Salvador in Transition.* Chapel Hill, N.C.: University of North Carolina Press, 1983.

Baloyra-Herp, Enrique. "The Persistent Conflict in El Salvador." *Current History* 90, no. 554 (Mar 1991): 121-124, 132-133.

Berryman, Phillip. *Inside Central America : The Essential Facts Past and Present on El Salvador, Nicaragua, Honduras, Guatemala, and Costa Rica.* 1st ed. New York: Pantheon Books, 1985.

Blanton, Shannon Lindsey. "Images in Conflict: The Case of Ronald Reagan and El Salvador." *International Studies Quarterly* 40, no. 1 (Mar. 1996): 23-44.

Bollinger, William. "Villalobos on "Popular Insurrection"." *Latin American Perspectives* 16, no. 3, Revolutionary Strategy in Central America (Summer 1989): 38-47.

Bosch, Brian J. *The Salvadoran Officer Corps and the Final Offensive of 1981.* Jefferson, NC: McFarland, 1999.

Buergenthal, Thomas. "Truth Commissions: Between Impunity and Prosecution." *Case Western Reserve Journal of International Law* 38, no. 2 (2006/2007): 217-223.

Bulmer-Thomas, V. "Economic Development Over the Long Run. Central America Since 1920." *Journal of Latin American Studies* 15, no. 2 (Nov. 1983): 269-294.

Byrne, Hugh Gregory. *El Salvador's Civil War: A Study of Revolution.* Boulder, CO: Lynne Rienner Publishers, 1996.

Carothers, Thomas. "Promoting Democracy and Fighting Terror." *Foreign Affairs*, January/February 2003. http://www. foreignaffairs.org/20030101faessay10224-p20/thomas-carothers/promoting-democracy-and-fighting-terror.html [accessed February 15, 2008].

Chernick, Marc W. "Negotiated Settlement to Armed Conflict: Lessons from the Colombian Peace Process." *Journal of Interamerican Studies and World Affairs* 30, no. 4 (Winter 1988): 53-88.

Carpenter, Ted Galen, "U.S. Aid to Anti-Communist Rebels: The "Reagan Doctrine" and its Pitfalls." The Cato Institute. http://www.cato.org/pubs/pas/pa074es.html. [accessed November 21, 2007].

Colburn, Forrest D. "The Fading of the Revolutionary Era in Central America." *Current History* 91, no. 562 (Feb 1992): 70-73.

Connell-Smith, Gordon. "Latin America in the Foreign Relations of the United States." *Journal of Latin American Studies* 8, no. 1 (May 1976): 137-150.

Department of Social Sciences Universidad de El Salvador. "An Analysis of the Correlation of Forces in El Salvador." *Latin American Perspectives* 14, no. 4, Contemporary Issues (Autumn 1987): 426-452.

DeRosa, Marshall L. *The Confederate Constitution of 1861: An Inquiry into American Constitutionalism*. Columbia, Missouri: University of Missouri Press, 1991.

Economist Intelligence Unit ViewsWire. *El Salvador: Ten-year growth outlook*. New York. July 13, 2007.

"El Salvador Civil War." Global Security. http://www.globalsecurity.org/military/world/war/elsalvador2.htm [accessed November 21, 2007].

El Salvador, 1979-1989: A Briefing Book on U.S. Aid and the Situation in El Salvador. Library of Congress. Congressional Research Service. (1990).

Etheredge, Lloyd S. *Can Governments Learn? : American Foreign Policy and Central American Revolutions*. New York: Pergamon Press, 1985.

Fagen, Richard R. *Forging Peace : The Challenge of Central America*. New York, NY: B. Blackwell, 1987.

Farer, Tom J. *U.S. Ends and Means in Central America: A Debate*. New York: Plenum Press, 1988.

Fenwick, C. G. "Procedure Under the Rio Treaty of Reciprocal Assistance." *The American Journal of International Law* 63, no. 4 (Oct. 1969): 769-770.

Foley, Michael W. "Laying the Groundwork: The Struggle for Civil Society in El Salvador." *Journal of Interamerican Studies and World Affairs* 38, no. 1 (Spring 1996): 67-104.

Gambone, Michael D. 2001. *Documents of American Diplomacy: From the American Revolution to the Present*. Westport, CT: Praeger Publishers. http://psi.praeger.com/doc.aspx?newindex =1&q=Monroe+Doctrine&c=&imageField.x=9&imageField.y=6&d=/books/dps/2000accd/2 000accd-p2000accd9970091002.xml&i=12. [accessed 16 November 2007].

Garcia, Jose Z. "Tragedy in El Salvador." *Current History* 89, no. 543 (Jan 1990): 9-12, 40.

Godwin, Jack. 2008. *The Arrow and the Olive Branch*. Westport, CT: Praeger Publishers. http:// psi.praeger.com/doc.aspx?newindex=1&q=Monroe+Doctrine&c=&imageField.x=9&image Field.y=6&d=/books/dps/2000accd/2000accd-p2000accd9970136001.xml&i=7. [accessed November 16, 2007].

Holiday, David. "El Salvador's "Model" Democracy." *Current History* 104, no. 679 (Feb 2005): 77-82.

Hooper, Glen, "Undermining Democracy," *The Globe and Mail,* December 24, 1988.

Hufford, Larry. "The U. S. in Central America: The Obfuscation of History." *Journal of Peace Research* 22, no. 2 (Jun. 1985): 93-100.

Huntington, Samuel P. "Will More Countries Become Democratic?" *Political Science Quarterly* 99, no. 2 (Summer 1984): 193-218.

Hurwitz, Jon, and Mark Peffley. "How are Foreign Policy Attitudes Structured? A Hierarchical Model." *The American Political Science Review* 81, no. 4 (Dec. 1987): 1099-1120.

Jacoby, Tamar, "The Reagan Turnaround on Human Rights," Foreign Affairs, http://www.foreignaffairs.org/19860601faessay7802/tamar-jacoby/the-reagan-turnaround-on-human-rights.html [accessed November 21, 2007].

Johnson, Robert H. "Misguided Morality: Ethics and the Reagan Doctrine." *Political Science Quarterly* 103, no. 3 (Autumn 1988): 509-529.

Jones, Errol D. "Militarization and Demilitarization in El Salvador's Transition to Democracy." *Journal of the West* 39, no. 1 (Jan 2000): 103.

Kaye, Mike. "The Role of Truth Commissions in the Search for Justice, Reconciliation and Democratisation: The Salvadorean and Honduran Cases." *Journal of Latin American Studies* 29, no. 3 (Oct. 1997): 693-716.

Kincaid, A. Douglas. "Demilitarization and Security in El Salvador and Guatemala: Convergences of Success and Crisis." *Journal of Interamerican Studies and World Affairs* 42, no. 4, Special Issue: Globalization and Democratization in Guatemala (Winter 2000): 39-58.

Kowalchuk, Lisa. "Asymmetrical Alliances, Organizational Democracy and Peasant Protest in El Salvador*." *The Canadian Review of Sociology and Anthropology* 40, no. 3 (Aug 2003): 291-309.

Krauss, Clifford. *Inside Central America : Its People, Politics, and History.* New York: Touchstone, 1991.

LaFeber, Walter. *Inevitable Revolutions : The United States in Central America.* Expand ed. New York: W.W. Norton, 1984.

Landrey, Wilbur G., "A Shambles in Central America," *St.Petersburg Times,* March 31, 1988.

Leiken, Robert S., ed. *Central America : Anatomy of Conflict.* New York: Pergamon Press, 1984.

LeoGrande, William M. *Our Own Backyard : The United States in Central America, 1977-1992.* Chapel Hill, NC: University of North Carolina Press, 1998.

------. "A Splendid Little War: Drawing the Line in El Salvador." *International Security* 6, no. 1 (Summer 1981): 27-52.

Little, Walter. "International Conflict in Latin America." *International Affairs (Royal Institute of International Affairs 1944-)* 63, no. 4 (Autumn 1987): 589-601.

Lowy, Michael, Eder Sader, and Stephen Gorman. "The Militarization of the State in Latin America." *Latin American Perspectives* 12, no. 4, State and Military in Latin America (Autumn 1985): 7-40.

Lumpkin, John J., "Rumsfeld Hoping Iraq is another El Salvador," *Deseret News,* November 12, 2004.

Manwaring, Max G. and Court Prisk, *El Salvador at War: An Oral History of Conflict from the 1979 Insurrection to the Present.* Washington, D.C.: National Defense University Press,1988.

Marcella, Gabriel. "The Latin American Military, Low Intensity Conflict, and Democracy." *Journal of Interamerican Studies and World Affairs* 32, no. 1 (Spring 1990): 45-82.

Mason, T. David. "The Civil War in El Salvador: A Retrospective Analysis." *Latin American Research Review* 34, no. 3 (1999): 179-196.

Montgomery, Tommie Sue. *Revolution in El Salvador: From Civil Strife to Civil Peace.* 2nd ed. Boulder: Westview Press, 1995.

Moore, John J.,Jr. "Problems with Forgiveness: Granting Amnesty Under the Arias Plan in Nicaragua and El Salvador." *Stanford Law Review* 43, no. 3 (Feb 1991): 733.

Nef, Jorge. "The Trend Toward Democratization and Redemocratization in Latin America: Shadow and Substance." *Latin American Research Review* 23, no. 3 (1988): 131-153.

O'Shaughnessy, Laura Nuzzi, and Michael Dodson. "Political Bargaining and Democratic Transitions: A Comparison of Nicaragua and El Salvador." *Journal of Latin American Studies* 31, no. 1 (Feb. 1999): 99-127.

"Oligarchy of Terrorism." *Boston Globe,* May 25, 1981.

Paige, Jeffery M. "Land Reform and Agrarian Revolution in El Salvador: Comment on Seligson and Diskin." *Latin American Research Review* 31, no. 2 (1996): 127-139.

------. "Coffee and Power in El Salvador." *Latin American Research Review* 28, no. 3 (1993): 7-40.

Pastor, Robert A. "Explaining U.S. Policy Toward the Caribbean Basin: Fixed and Emerging Images." *World Politics* 38, no. 3 (Apr. 1986): 483-515.

------. "Continuity and Change in U.S. Foreign Policy: CARTER AND REAGAN ON EL SALVADOR." *Journal of Policy Analysis & Management* 3, no. 2 (Winter 1984): 175-190.

Pearce, Jenny. *Under the Eagle: U.S. Intervention in Central America and the Caribbean.* 1ST U.S. ed. Boston, Ma: South End Press, 1982.

Pfaff, William, "U.S. Makes Mistakes when Ideology Prevails," *The Ottawa Citizen,* December 28, 1989.

Power, Jonathan, "Commentary; this Time, Stay Out of Nicaragua's Affairs," *Los Angeles Times,* November 2, 2001.

Quan, Adan. "Through the Looking Glass: U.S. Aid to El Salvador and the Politics of National Identity." *American Ethnologist* 32, no. 2 (May 2005): 276-293.

Radu, Michael. "Latin America -- El Salvador at War: An Oral History Edited by Max G. Manwaring and Court Prisk." *Orbis* 33, no. 3 (Summer 1989): 478.

Ribando, Claire. "El Salvador: Political, Economic, and Social Conditions and Relations with the United States." Library of Congress Congressional Research Service (updated May 3, 2005). http://www.fas.org/sgp/crs/row/RS21655.pdf [accessed on November 18, 2007].

Robinson, Linda, "Playing by our Rules," *New York Times,* December 29, 1991.

Roht-Arriaza, Naomi, and Lauren Gibson. "The Developing Jurisprudence on Amnesty." *Human Rights Quarterly* 20, no. 4 (Nov 1998): 843.

Schorow, Stephanie, "El Salvador's Long History of Torment," *Boston Herald,* May 23, 2001.

Schulzinger, Robert D. "Foreign Policy." *American Quarterly* 35, no. 1/2, Special Issue: Contemporary America (Spring - Summer 1983): 39-58.

Seligson, Mitchell A. "Thirty Years of Transformation in the Agrarian Structure of El Salvador, 1961-1991." *Latin American Research Review* 30, no. 3 (1995): 43-74.

Sharpe, Kenneth E. "The Post-Vietnam Formula Under Siege: The Imperial Presidency and Central America." *Political Science Quarterly* 102, no. 4 (Winter 1987): 549-569.

Singelmann, Peter. "Campesino Movements and Class Conflict in Latin America: The Functions of Exchange and Power." *Journal of Interamerican Studies and World Affairs* 16, no. 1 (Feb. 1974): 39-72.

Slater, Jerome. "Dominos in Central America: Will they Fall? Does it Matter?" *International Security* 12, no. 2 (Autumn 1987): 105-134.

Smyth, Frank. "Consensus or Crisis? Without Duarte in El Salvador." *Journal of Interamerican Studies and World Affairs* 30, no. 4 (Winter 1988): 29-52.

Sobel, Richard. "A Report: Public Opinion about United States Intervention in El Salvador and Nicaragua." *The Public Opinion Quarterly* 53, no. 1 (Spring 1989): 114-128.

Soderlund, Walter C. "A Comparison of Press Coverage in Canada and the United States of the 1982 and 1984 Salvadoran Elections." *Canadian Journal of Political Science / Revue Canadienne De Science Politique* 23, no. 1 (Mar. 1990): 59-72.

Stahler-Sholk, Richard. "El Salvador's Negotiated Transition: From Low-Intensity Conflict to Low-Intensity Democracy." *Journal of Interamerican Studies and World Affairs* 36, no. 4 (Winter 1994): 1-59.

Steinfels, Margaret O'Brien. "Death and Lies in El Salvador: The Ambassador's Tale." Creighton University. http://www.creighton.edu/CollaborativeMinistry/RbtWhite.html [accessed December 20, 2007].

Stokes, William S. "Violence as a Power Factor in Latin-American Politics." *The Western Political Quarterly* 5, no. 3 (Sep. 1952): 445-468.

Summerfield, Derek. "Unspeakable Truths: Confronting State Terror and Attrocity." *British Medical Journal* 323, no. 7321 (November 10, 2001): 1135.

"Transcript of President's Speech on Central America Policy," *New York Times,* May 10, 1984.

The Truth about El Salvador, December 1990. Puntarenas, Costa Rica: S.N., 1990.

U.S. Congress. House. Committee on Foreign Affairs. Subcommittee on Western Hemisphere. *El Salvador: Status of Reconstruction Activities One Year after the Peace Agreement.*

Statement of Harold J. Johnson, U.S. General Accounting Office. GAO/T-NSIAD-93-10 (1993): 13.

United States Department of State's Bureau of International Information Programs. "Monroe Doctrine (1823)." United States Department of State International Information Programs. http://usinfo. state.gov/usa/infousa/facts/democrac/50.htm; accessed November 16, 2007.

Valis, Noël. "Fear and Torment in El Salvador." *The Massachusetts Review* 48, no. 1 (Spring 2007): 117.

Vanderlaan, Mary. "The Dual Strategy Myth in Central American Policy." *Journal of Interamerican Studies and World Affairs* 26, no. 2 (May 1984): 199-224.

Vilas, Carlos M. "Prospects for Democratisation in a Post-Revolutionary Setting: Central America." *Journal of Latin American Studies* 28, no. 2 (May 1996): 461-503.

Walter, Knut, and Philip J. Williams. "The Military and Democratization in El Salvador." *Journal of Interamerican Studies and World Affairs* 35, no. 1 (1993): 39-88.

Weeks, John. "An Interpretation of the Central American Crisis." *Latin American Research Review* 21, no. 3 (1986): 31-53.

Whitehead, Laurence. "Explaining Washington's Central American Policies." *Journal of Latin American Studies* 15, no. 2 (Nov. 1983): 321-363.

Wood, Elisabeth Jean. *Forging Democracy from Below: Insurgent Transitions in South Africa and El Salvador.* Cambridge, UK ; New York: Cambridge University Press, 2000.